MAKING
THE MOST OF
SMALL
SPACES

MAKING
THE MOST OF
SMALL
SPACES

ANOOP PARIKH

RIZZOLI
NEW YORK

FOR MY FAMILY, AND DAVID

First published in the United States of America in 1994 by
RIZZOLI INTERNATIONAL PUBLICATIONS, INC.
300 Park Avenue South, New York, NY10010

First published in Great Britain in 1994 by
Conran Octopus Limited

Reprinted in 2000

Project Editor   Joanna Bradshaw
Art Editor   Helen Lewis
Designer   Christine Wood
Picture Research   Jessica Walton
Production   Mano Mylvaganam
Illustrator   Sarah John

LC No: 93-87090

ISBN 0-8478-1801-2

Printed in china

CONTENTS

BASICS

In order to make the most of your home you need to identify the activities that take place within it. Only then can you accommodate them in the most efficient and stylish way.

Think about the ways in which you might reorganize the space to make the most of what you have, by altering the function of each room or its storage arrangements for example. You can also make it appear larger, through clever use of color, light, and texture and a careful choice of furniture.

PLANNING

- Draw up scale plans of your home and decide whether any structural alterations are appropriate.
- Are there any original features that you want to keep or replace, such as fireplaces, built-in cabinets or plasterwork?
- Think about how much time and money you have at your disposal.
- Are you a keen or reluctant home decorator?
- Check the condition of walls, floors, ceilings, and windows.
- Decide whether you want to emphasize or minimize the view.
- Work out at what time of the day each room gets the sun and for how long.
- Work out your space priorities by deciding which of the following are most important to you: a work and hobbies space; a private refuge; all-purpose family rooms; a space in which to entertain; separate rooms for each occupant; or more than one bathroom.

FIRST THINGS FIRST

For the vast majority of people, small living spaces are the norm, the inevitable consequence of sky-high land values and a strong demand for individual living units.

It is possible to create stylish small spaces, but it is not always easy to feel inspired by a room or apartment that is the size of your average broom closet. The hardest part is knowing where to begin. Ask yourself "What do I really want?" Think about how your home fits into your lifestyle; if it helps, make a checklist of each room's main features to establish your priorities.

If your home is the place where you both live and work, your needs will be different from those of someone who uses theirs as a crash pad. Similarly, if you live alone, you will have the luxury of only having to please yourself. A couple or a family will have further demands to make on a limited living area, so tailor your plans accordingly.

However small a living space, your first step should be to draw up scale plans of your home. This gives you a useful map of the area, allows you to plan your decorative campaign, and helps to highlight any potential blackspots or awkward corners.

This all sounds deeply analytical, and nowhere near as interesting as someone pronouncing that "pink is always fabulous in a south-facing room". But there is nothing less fabulous than a room whose use is ill defined. Better to decide in advance, for example, that you are going to combine the living room and bedroom, so that you can have a kitchen that is large enough to entertain in. Or, to realize from the outset that there is no need for a separate study because you are much happier working on the kitchen table.

Take a critical look at your present arrangements. Are you hanging on to bulky furniture simply because it was cheap and it is still in one piece? If you never eat breakfast, do you really need a toaster? To edit the contents of your home costs nothing, and it may be all you need to create additional and more efficient living space in a small area.

Decorating is not just about planning and organizing rooms, it is also about creating the right atmosphere by making the best use of color, pattern, light, and texture. This is where other people's efforts come into their own. Successful small spaces that have been carefully designed are the most potent source of inspiration for anyone wishing to plan their own home, so sift through magazines and books for ideas to suit your individual needs.

If you have ever spent time in a beach hut (opposite) or on a boat, you will know that small spaces have a charm all of their own.

Most of us would abandon any thought of decorating and using a room of this size. However, it has taken only one or two interesting textures and a sentimental approach to furnishing to turn this seaside hut into a welcoming retreat.

A lack of space often prompts us to come up with wonderfully creative design solutions: A console table in this sleekly furnished studio (left) doubles as a dressing table, and an etched glass screen lets light dance around the room, while maintaining a sense of enclosure in the living area.

An aerial view of a simply furnished open-plan studio (previous page, left) shows a successful combination of plain color and natural materials in a small space.

In a minimal interior (previous page, right), bold and simple storage units attached to the wall are both practical and decorative.

A GOOD USE OF SPACE

- Place your furniture according to where it makes the most economical and creative use of space.

- Do not automatically exclude large items of furniture from a tiny space. An oversized, attractive piece can be an excellent focal point in a small, enclosed room.

- Consider using "enlarging devices" such as mirrors and monochrome color schemes. A minimal approach to furniture and soft furnishings will also make a room seem larger.

- In small houses, consider converting the basement or attic, or adding onto the back of the building to extend the living area.

- Think about your storage requirements and how best to incorporate them into your overall plan. Do not forget that even shallow recesses and awkward corners can be put to good use. Fit them out with shelves to provide storage and display space.

- Why waste the space above your head? A narrow shelf at picture rail height can be used to display decorative items or collections.

HIDDEN ASSETS

A simple archway (right) frames the view into a minimally-furnished sleeping area, while a sweep of drapery provides a dramatic and space-efficient alternative to double doors. Archways, like screens, help to define and separate spaces. They can also add elegance to a room that has less than perfect proportions.

Architectural features are best kept simple in small spaces, as ornate designs can easily overwhelm a room. Besides, it is seldom possible to stand back and appreciate them.

Sleeping areas can be hidden from view by placing them above eye level (left). The addition of a platform at one end of this high-ceilinged room effectively creates two more rooms: a small bathroom below, and a cosy bedroom above. The framework supporting the platform also incorporates plenty of useful built-in cabinets.

In tight spaces, ladders conserve more space than staircases. As well as being more compact, they are much cheaper, and can easily be stored in a corner when not in use. However, high level areas that are in constant use are best reached by fixed stairs.

LET THE SPACE SPEAK

A dramatic triple-height space makes it difficult to believe that the total floor area of this one-bedroom house (left) is only 540 square feet. On the first floor, a folding wall provides useful screening in the living area, where the kitchen space extends right under the stairs. The second level houses the bathroom, which receives daylight via a translucent panel. The landing can be used as a study area thanks to a built-in desk, while the floor above contains a compact double bedroom, complete with built-in closets.

To compensate for the lack of space, high-quality finishes and fittings have been used. In small homes, minor elements, such as taps and handrails, are much more visible, and therefore have more impact, so choose the best quality fittings you can afford. They will make a big difference.

The opposite is true of this bathroom (right) which was once a closet. A rich yellow wall, cosy and bright, is perfectly counterpointed by a frame of midnight-blue woodwork, the vivid colors helping to mask basic fittings and less than perfect finishing. The tiny floor area provides just enough space for a traditional bath, which is boxed in with tongue-and-groove paneling to echo the closet's original lining. This kind of paneling is especially suitable for traditional bathrooms. Additional shelf space can be created by providing a narrow 4-inch ledge on top of the boarding. Wooden surrounds like this should always be sealed with several coats of yacht varnish after painting to counteract the effects of water and steam.

USING COLOR

- Daytime rooms look best painted in light, airy colors, to make them look bigger.
- If you are lucky enough to have sun for much of the day, a color scheme based on blue and green is a fresh-looking option.
- If a room looks gray and dingy, perhaps because it faces north, use a warm color such as soft yellow, or a shot of lime green.
- Night-time rooms are a good place to try out strong, dark colors. They make a room seem more formal, but are better suited to the warm glow of candles and electric light.
- To "lower" a high ceiling, try painting it two or three shades darker than the walls. To "raise" a low ceiling, use a pale, cool color. Painting the end wall of a narrow room in a strong color will make it appear wider and nearer.
- Color can be used to create separate areas within a room. You can define and "anchor" the living area with a colorful rug or, to make spaces flow smoothly into one another, use similar intensities of color in adjoining areas.

GEOMETRIC GLAMOUR

Blocks of color and a square motif provide a strong yet simple theme for this 310 square foot second-floor studio, while an elegantly curved wall dispels the boxy feeling so often experienced in small spaces.

The wall was designed to ensure that the kitchen and bathroom (right) occupied a tiny amount of floor space. Much of the kitchen is hidden behind sliding doors when not in use, and the small area that remains permanently on show has been decorated to blend in with its surroundings. Lighting is provided by pivoting low-voltage halogen spots. They produce a whiter light than conventional bulbs, which makes them eminently suitable for lighting large expanses of color.

By placing the bathroom next to the kitchen, ugly runs of plumbing are kept to a minimum. Where there is no room even for a shower tray, as here, it is a good idea to fix the shower unit to the wall and insert a drainage hole in the floor. Marble and mosaic tiles work especially well, as they are decorative as well as hardwearing. They are also a relatively cheap flooring solution for a small area.

Unlike an ordinary partition wall, the

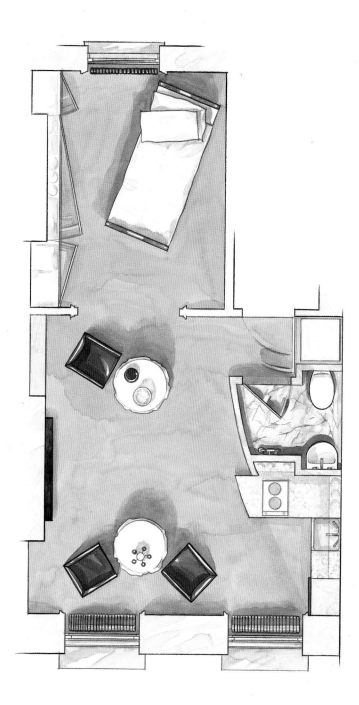

curved wall stops well below the ceiling. This makes it less obtrusive, and enables the top to be used for storage (right). As the platform gets only occasional use, a folding stepladder is used to gain access.

Built-in storage is provided by shelves hidden behind huge doors (above right). For lightness, these are made from artists' canvas stretched over wooden frames.

In the living area (above left), shutters provide a crisp alternative to draperies. A sheet trimmed at one end to make a decorative pelmet softens the mood in the sleeping area. It also helps to screen an ugly view.

The blue ceiling brings the outside in, and provides a dramatic contrast to the white walls and neutral floor. Additionally, it ensures that the apartment stands out from its neighbors when seen from the outside.

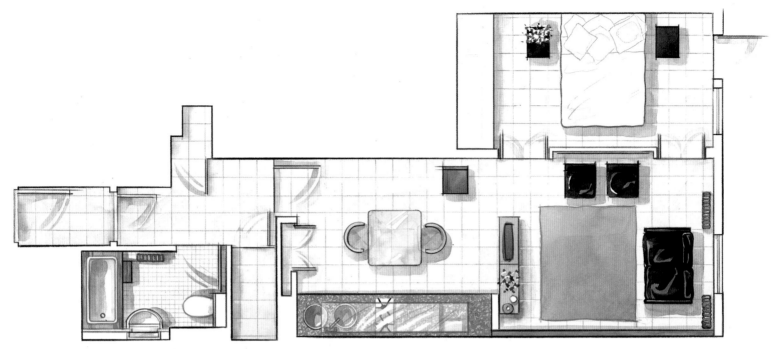

LESS IS MORE

In this tiny one-bedroom apartment, a lack of architectural detail has been turned into a positive feature by the adoption of a pared-down approach to decoration. Two boxy rooms were opened up to create one large living area (right and opposite), leaving just enough space for a double bedroom (far right).

Modern chairs, abstract art, and plain ceramics are a natural choice for such a rectilinear space. The tiled floor makes the room feel wider, while blocks of bold color act as focal points.

Lighting is equally streamlined: Background light is provided by low-voltage fittings behind a wooden fin.

THE LAYERED LOOK

A surprising number of distinct spaces
have been shoehorned into this apartment, thanks to the owner's ingenious
use of half-levels and steps.

The full height of the space can be
seen in the living area (left), with its
symmetrically-placed sofas and dining
furniture, all on castors. A desire for
symmetry also determined the position
of the kitchen, which lines up with the
entrance stairs. It is emphasized by a
pair of monumental steps, which double
up as kitchen drawers (right).

The drawers, together with most of
the woodwork, are colorwashed to
create a subtle striped effect that tones
with the fabric used throughout for
screening and soft furnishings. It also
"raises" the low ceilings.

Elsewhere, the space is divided horizontally into several levels. The main
sleeping area was created by building a
platform over the stairs and galley. A
second bedroom and bath (center
right) have been slotted into one of the
rooms that leads off the main space,
while the area under the bed and the
steps leading up to the bath have been
used to create extra storage.

If you were to climb the steps next
to the bath, you would suddenly find

yourself on the lower bed in the narrow
room (above). There is just enough
room to clamber onto the floor on the
other side, and from here it is but a
short climb up the ladder into a
nautical-style box bed.

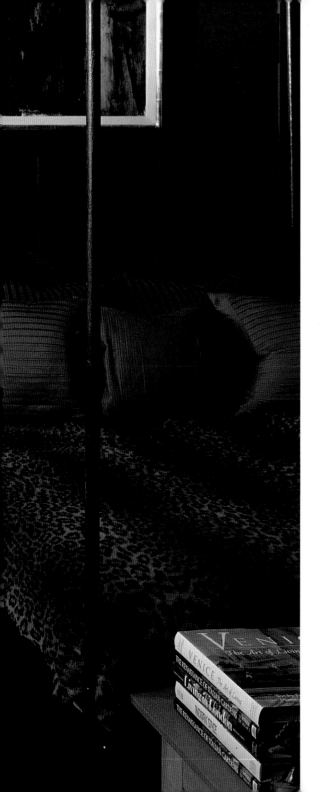

ONE-ROOM LIVING

Fitting a wide range of activities and services into one small room is possible – you just have to make imaginative and efficient use of the space. There are two main approaches: The first consists of keeping the room as open as possible. Furniture is kept to a minimum and arranged around the edges of the room. The alternative is to divide the space into areas of activity, using screening, decorative materials, and changes in floor level. Whichever you choose, the result should be easy to use.

ALL IN ONE

In theory at least, life in a studio or a small apartment has much to recommend it. Small spaces are cheap to buy or rent, heating bills are low, they take less time to clean, and, with a bit of careful thought, you can even end up with a truly labor-saving home.

Plenty of single people, couples, and even families live, sleep, eat, and entertain in just one room; in several of the world's major cities, there is simply no other option. However, few would deny that it takes some planning. And many are overwhelmed, if not thoroughly defeated, by the challenge of creating a stylish, as well as practical, small home.

So how do you do it? You keep it simple, that's how. The best-looking studios are invariably those that make the most of one or two good design ideas. These can be practical, such as a wall of cabinets that even includes the kitchen sink, or decorative - practically every surface in the studio on page 20,for example, is covered in a rich emerald green fabric, a wonderfully grand way of excluding the outside world.

It also helps to restrict your color palette, perhaps to several closely related tones of the same color. You are less likely to tire of restful and neutral schemes, and it is very easy to introduce small amounts of a stronger or contrasting color as an accent. This could be in the form of cushions, throws, or vases of flowers.

While wall and floor surfaces should be tough enough to cope with around-the-clock use, they should also provide a suitably plain backdrop for furniture, rugs, and pictures.

In addition, floors need to feel warm and comfortable underfoot, and they should be easy to clean.

However, your first task is to organize the space. The room's shape will help you do this, especially if there are changes of level, perhaps in the form of a gallery, and fixed points of interest, such as windows or a fireplace. The position of the kitchen may well be determined by the location of the existing water supply, and the need to site extractor fans near an outside wall.

Even if you are starting from scratch, it is a good idea to incorporate changes of level in the design, because this is the best way to define each area in a room. Alternatively, position large pieces of furniture so that they create a sense of separation without blocking the

OPEN HOUSE

A change in level turns one room into several separate spaces in this bright studio apartment (right). Open stairs lead to a galleried sleeping and study area (left), and structural elements are left exposed to create a simple, stripped-back-to-basics feel. Much of this room's charm derives from being able to see from one area to another. Painting everything white gives the space an enviable freshness, but there are plenty of small, and not-so-small, patches of bright color for the eye to alight upon.

Where there is a greater sense of enclosure, as in a galleried studio (previous page, right), wood tones focus your attention on the architecture and furniture. In another studio (previous page, left), rich colors and fabrics help to create a glamorous and sophisticated mood.

BOLD EXPOSURE

Giving a room a strong focal point may take some courage, but it always pays dividends. In this converted barn, a stove fulfills its traditional role, that of an efficient heat source for every part of the home. Siting it centrally also helps to create several distinct but informal areas in one room.

The sunken living area is given a greater sense of enclosure by the addition of a turned and painted column, which supports the sleeping platform above. The bulk of the stove also draws the eye away from the neatly recessed kitchen and dining table beyond.

A sense of unity prevails because, as far as possible, the same materials and colors have been used throughout.

While large items of furniture make splendid focal points, they can be heavy. Here, two slabs of granite are used to protect the pine floor.

view. Screens and arches are a more elegant way of doing much the same thing.

The largest and most important pieces of furniture in any studio are those that you sit and sleep on. In many cases, of course, these are one and the same; most studio dwellers opt for some form of sofa bed or foldaway. The room's layout should make the switch from living room to bedroom, and back again, as effortless as possible; this means keeping the area in front of the sofa or folding bed clear, and providing storage for bedlinen. If all this sounds too much like hard work, some form of daybed may well be the answer.

Whatever you choose to sleep on, make sure it is built to provide adequate back support. Sofa beds made from blocks of foam are not suitable for much more than occasional use. Instead, look for a sofa bed mechanism that has a slatted base and a pocket-sprung mattress. The best types ensure that the mattress will fold without exerting undue pressure at the point of the fold. Futons, which contain layers of cotton wadding, are equally suitable; in fact, many people prefer their solid feel, and they are available in an increasing variety of designs.

The number and size of windows in a room will also influence the layout. If you have a wonderful view, it makes sense to position the furniture so that you can enjoy it at all times. Even if the room does not benefit from a view, windows are best left clear; this helps to make the most of natural light, and makes closing the draperies or blinds much easier. However, there are times when you can't avoid placing furniture in front of the windows. If this is the case, try to keep it as low and unobtrusive as you possibly can.

STUDIO LAYOUT

- Do you want to keep the room as open as possible? Or would you prefer to divide it into several smaller areas? Is there a change of level or is it possible, or necessary, to create one?

- Are there items of furniture that can be used as focal points or screening? Screens can be mysterious as well as practical, enticing you to discover what lies behind them.

- Use the walls for display, storage, lighting, and heating.

- Take a careful look at your sleeping arrangements. Can the sofa bed or futon be made up in a hurry? Are you prepared to stow away the bed and the bedlinen every morning?

- You could opt for a bed that remains on view, but it is rarely a good idea to allow it to dominate the room. A studio that looks too much like a bedroom can make visitors feel as though they are intruding.

- Keep eating and cooking areas close together to reduce the risk of accidents, and make sure that there is good ventilation. If possible, try to screen the kitchen from general view. Then you will feel less guilty about dirty dishes.

L-SHAPED LIVING

Custom-built cooking, sleeping, dining, and living areas slot into this L-shaped room with enviable precision (left). One branch of the "L" has been divided horizontally in two by a sleeping platform. But it looks anything but cramped, because your eye is swept up by the lines of the built-in storage that runs from floor to ceiling. The shelves below the sleeping platform are used for display, while the cabinets above help to hide pillows and other bedlinen. Only the neatly rolled futon remains on permanent show.

A platform can be hung on brackets, as here, or it can be cantilevered off the walls, or supported on columns. These veneered columns are more decorative than structural, however. One forms part of the ladder up to the bed, and helps to disguise an ugly pillar; the other one is used as a wine rack and coat closet.

Extra chairs and accent lighting are hung on the wall as a neat storage solution. This leaves valuable table and floor space as clear as possible.

In the kitchen area, steel framing and toughened glass have been used to make a multipurpose yet sculptural island unit, complete with microwave

oven and an ingenious sink (left and above). This has the advantage of being much less obtrusive than conventional units. However, serious cooks should remember that a miniature sink or a low-level oven, like these, can soon become an irritant.

In direct contrast to the dramatic shapes and hard surfaces used elsewhere, the living space has a simple, restful feel. The whole area is raised slightly, and squashy cushions are propped up against the walls to create comfortable, casual seating. The all-white scheme is softened by a background wash of blue light produced by fittings concealed in the columns. To make reading easier, a pool of clear light is provided by a pendant fitting which also acts as a focal point.

Clutter often jars in simply decorated rooms, so books are kept hidden, and dust-free, behind tailor-made shutter-style cabinet doors.

DIVIDING SPACE

A low wall neatly solves the problem of making one room perform several functions. The owners of this studio badly needed to create more space in the bathroom, which occupies the area beyond the tinted glass door. But they were reluctant to move the existing wall, partly because their budget would not allow it, but also because it would have cut across the room's best features – namely the run of full-length windows and the gently vaulted ceiling.

The solution was to build a low wall or screen to section off part of the living room, and to hide the sink and towels behind it. This created more space in the bathroom, and made the morning rush a little easier to handle. The lines of the windows and ceiling remain unbroken and the seating area feels more welcoming.

The new addition was positioned to allow for plenty of movement around the bathroom door. It also follows the line of the built-in closets, which helps to integrate it into the existing layout of the room.

MANAGING CLUTTER

Mirrors and a pale, neutral color scheme will make a room look bigger, but they are much less effective if the place is untidy. Well-planned storage is a must in any small space, and some form of built-in unit could be the answer. Tailored shelves and drawers make excellent use of a large alcove (left); they extend right across the space to include even the window recess. However, care has been taken to ensure that the unit looks like a piece of furniture. The shelves are encased in a frame, and the central section made deeper to create a break-front effect. This provides sufficient depth for the television, and lends the unit greater charm.

There are, however, more casual ways of displaying collected treasures. Massed pictures and market-finds jostle for space with rich textiles and antique furniture in this Parisian apartment (right). At first glance, the space seems merely chaotic, but the owner's talent for creating interesting groups of objects lends it a coherent unity.

DISPLAY STORAGE

- Find a space for favorite items and keep them there. Objects of the same type, be they books, pictures, or china, make more of an impact when gathered in one place. In quantity, books also provide heat and noise insulation.

- Storage can become a decorative feature in its own right. Hang light chairs and cabinets on a wall, or off a Shaker-style peg rail. Or, store a television or hi-fi in a redundant fireplace.

- Which is better, freestanding or built-in shelving? Freestanding examples can be moved at a later date, and are often attractive objects, but they may not fit a space exactly.

- Built-in shelves make the best use of space, especially in awkward corners and in the space above doors and windows.

- If the wall behind open shelves is lined with mirror, it will make the objects placed on the shelves look more impressive. A mirror will also give the impression that the room continues behind it.

- Store delicate objects away from kitchen grease and steam.

CONCEALED STORAGE

- Try to find furniture that "disappears" when not in use but make sure it is easy to operate.
- Keep a large linen or log basket handy for instant tidy-ups when you have unexpected visitors.
- Fit recesses such as alcoves with adjustable shelves, hooks, and rails.
- Built-in storage blends easily into its surroundings. Treat tailored units in the same way as adjacent walls to make them seem less prominent.

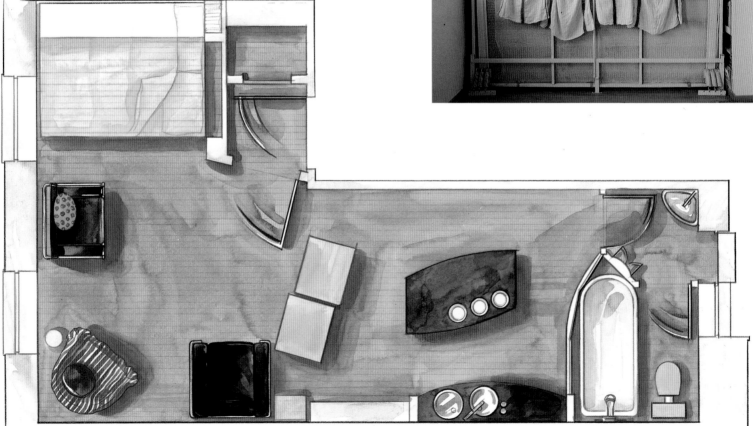

HOME ALONE

Sleeping space and a storage area are cleverly combined in this tiny city hideout. A foldaway bed, books, baskets, and even a clothesline, are hidden behind a large Venetian blind during the day. This allows the owner to deal instantly with clutter whenever it gets out of hand, and leaves the area free for living and working in.

Keeping furniture to a minimum makes it easy to effect the transformation, while the plain walls and maple floor foster a sense of calm.

Muted backdrops are often preferable in studio apartments; they increase the sense of space, and focus attention on decorative items. (Strong color and pattern are not forbidden though; if you use them with conviction throughout the space, they will work just as well.) The Venetian blind that covers the recess matches those at the windows, thereby subtly suggesting that there may be space, rather than clutter, behind. A mirror placed on the opposite wall is a more conventional way of "enlarging" a room.

BLUE BOX

There are times when lining furniture up against the walls can make your home look like a doctor's waiting room, but in certain circumstances this arrangement makes the best use of space. In this boxy 215 square foot studio, each wall is dominated by one large item of furniture: namely cabinets, a sofa bed, and a dining table that seats ten people.

Smaller items have been chosen for their lightness and flexibility. The low table and rattan armchair can easily be pushed out of the way when it is time for bed. And the perforated metal screen usefully hides kitchen mess during dinner parties.

Fresh blue walls give the space an ethereal quality, and provide a subtle tint for white surfaces such as the ceiling and curtains. They also contrast well with the warm wood tones, and the tough, polished surface of the concrete floor and steel lockers. The square lockers are particularly useful for storing clothes, as each can be used for different items. Their taller counterparts, meanwhile, are fitted with extra shelves to contain the hi-fi and books.

BENCH MARK

This wooden settle (right) serves several purposes. It mixes colors and textures in a sophisticated yet welcoming way and, with the aid of a thin mattress and scatter cushions, sits three people for dinner in comfort.

Once the table and dining chairs have been cleared away (the table top lifts easily from the base), it reverts to being an elegant, if slightly formal, sofa. It might be difficult to relax completely on such a rigid structure, but a sofa like this is an option worth considering if you entertain lots of guests regularly. This solution also works well in a lobby or hall.

Like many wooden objects, the settle enriches the simple, warm color scheme, and its clean lines let it blend well with more contemporary pieces. Splinters can sometimes be a problem with old wooden furniture, but it is possible to remove them with medium-grade sandpaper.

If you simply cannot face the thought of making and unmaking the bed twice a day, a cunningly disguised divan bed (opposite) is a good alternative. During the day, a simple cover in a hardwearing fabric hides the bed-linen, while bolsters, pillows, and

scatter cushions transform it into an extra-deep and inviting sofa. This arrangement suits casual and cluttered rooms best of all; it works less well in formal or minimal interiors.

Since you are aiming to make life easier, use fitted sheets and a quilt so that the bed can be made instantly. If there are drawers in the base, use them to store the quilt and extra linen. Also, turn the mattress regularly to even out wear and tear.

Sometimes, rooms resist your best efforts to keep them tidy, and the clutter simply takes on a life of its own. Here, a collection of pictures and other mementoes has spread to cover most of the walls and table surfaces, and the room feels darker and more cramped than it once was. But the richness of the overall effect more than makes up for any loss of light and space, and it gives the room character. Occasionally it pays to bend the rules.

MULTI-PURPOSE FURNITURE

- Sofas are not the only items of furniture that can be used as beds; it is also possible to buy upholstered footstools and ottomans containing sofa bed mechanisms. On some, the top lifts off to reveal a coffee table.

- Daybeds can be used for both seating and sleeping, and while they were designed to be placed against a wall, they work equally well when placed in the center of a room.

- A stool or chair that turns into steps is a necessary piece of furniture if you have tall bookshelves or high-level storage.

- Trunks and blanket chests can double up as storage spaces and low tables. A squab cushion placed on top will also provide occasional seating.

- The space in bay windows and other projecting windows works hardest when fitted with cabinets topped with a cushioned seat.

- Consider buying a dining table that can be lowered to coffee-table height.

- Use trolleys and butler's trays that double up as side tables.

MIRRORS AND SCREENS

■ Walls of mirror are great space expanders, but they need to be used with care. Avoid sitting people directly in front of them, as there is nothing more uncomfortable than continually catching sight of yourself. While covering one wall in mirror can seem to double the space in a room, if you use any more than this, strange multiple reflections will be created.

■ Built-in closet doors can sometimes be removed and replaced with sliding mirrored panels.

■ Use a folding screen to conjure up an instant dining area, workspace, or dressing room. It will hide your bed during the day, and replace draperies or blinds at night.

■ Making your own screen is surprisingly easy: Buy sheets of MDF (medium-density fiberboard) from hardware stores; good suppliers will cut these to size, as long as your demands are not too complex. Join the panels with screen hinges, then decorate with paint, paper, or fabric.

SCREEN STARS

The simple act of unfolding a screen bestows a sense of order in a tiny studio (left), and lends greater intimacy to a dining area (below). Screens have many practical uses including concealing clutter, but they are also extremely useful for adding drama to small or boxy rooms. Mirrors open up and extend spaces. In a dining area (right), objects placed in front of the mirror strengthen the impression of a room "beyond".

KITCHENS

Most kitchens are subject to a wide variety of uses, and the contemporary kitchen, in addition to looking good and being the place for regular food preparation, may also serve as a laundry, an office, and an entertainment area. If there is somewhere to sit, the room will quickly become the heart of your home.

However, if you never cook or eat at home, a conventional kitchen is a waste of space; a closet with a built-in refrigerator, rangetop, and microwave oven would make much more sense.

PLANNING

A well-planned kitchen, whatever its size, is one in which the food preparation areas, cooking facilities, and storage zones are all close at hand.

Professional planners begin by positioning the sink, range, and refrigerator so that the distances between them are kept to a minimum; these three points create what is known as the working triangle. Worktop space should be provided next to each point of the triangle, so that there is always somewhere to put food and utensils when you are cooking and preparing food.

The next step should be to analyze how you shop for, prepare, and serve your food. If you shop infrequently and seldom cook for more than one or two people, the design of your kitchen should reflect this, with plenty of space devoted to a pantry and a large freezer, and less room given over to pans and dishes. If, on the other hand, you entertain frequently and can shop every day, you will need plenty of counterspace and storage for tableware and saucepans, and less in the way of long-term food storage.

As always, compromises will have to be made. You may have to do without a full range of appliances, so choose those that do the jobs you hate most. There may not be room to store two sets of china, one for everyday use and one for entertaining, so select a design that will see you through every occasion.

The subject of storage is often made needlessly complicated. The golden rule should be to store items near to where they are most often used. In very small spaces, it is also a good idea to store as much as possible between

shoulder and hip height so as to avoid repeated bending and stretching in a confined area.

The insides of some built-in units make appalling use of space, but they can be improved by removing the central shelf and replacing it with a set of baskets on runners. If this is not possible, clip-on accessories, such as racks for glasses, are a good alternative.

As the worktop is the most accessible area in the room, it should be home only to those items that are in constant use, such as the coffee maker or knife blocks. It should not be used for displaying decorative clutter which can become extremely irritating if you need space for preparing an elaborate meal.

FIT TO WORK

The fitted versus unfitted storage debate rages loudest in the kitchen. Some people insist that only built-in units make the best use of space. Others point to the charm and durability of traditional freestanding furniture. The most sensible option seems to be a mixture of the two. In this basement kitchen (left), a run of units with built-in appliances is easier to clean than old-fashioned cabinets and a range. But traces of tradition remain, in the form of a quarry-tiled floor and a farmhouse-style table. The fireplace serves as the focal point of the room.

In a country kitchen (right), a butcher's block provides a sturdy yet movable work surface and stops the sofa from looking as though it has been marooned in the middle of the room. Meanwhile, a chest of drawers and sideboard slot neatly into the wall space.

Massed banks of fitted cabinets are rarely the answer for a small kitchen, because the framework and doors take up too much space. As the kitchens on the previous page show, you are much better off with shelves, rails, and plenty of hooks to hang things on in a small space. Enjoy making a virtue out of displaying kitchen items.

HANGING AROUND

Open storage gives this galley kitchen (left) a functional yet welcoming feel. Although the owner's penchant for all things fishy creates a welcome touch of whimsy, the kitchen's greatest strength is its layout; everything can be located, used, and returned to its proper place with a minimum of fuss.

This area is also a thoroughfare, so fragile items are stored well back or high up to reduce the risk of being knocked, and open shelves are made more secure with the addition of thin fabric rails. The whole area is painted a dark color to disguise the fact that it consists of several units, and to help make a decorative feature of the items displayed. Wall-mounted faucets leave the sink area clear.

In this 17 square foot kitchen (right), stainless steel, white tiling, and bright color provide an equally dramatic backdrop. Hanging baskets and a suspended shelf are used to keep precious counterspace clear of clutter, while delicate and heavy items are safely stored in pull-out cabinets or on low-level shelves.

STORAGE AND DISPLAY

- In very tight spaces, MDF (medium-density fiberboard) panels set in sliding door tracks can be used to replace conventional cabinet doors. Alternatively, hide storage shelves behind washable fabric drapes hung on plastic-coated wire. Measure the width of the cabinet, and double the figure to work out the amount of fabric needed.

- Short lengths of plastic-coated wire can be fixed inside cabinet doors to hold saucepan lids in place. This makes them easier to find, and creates more space inside for larger items.

- Corner cabinets are often the worst culprits when it comes to wasted space, but they can be improved if fitted with turntable baskets and shelves that swing out when the door is opened.

- Open shelves for food and utensils should be located away from steamy areas, such as the sink and range. However, siting a plate rack near the sink can remove the need for a draining board. A wall-mounted rack fixed over the rangetop can be used to warm plates and serving dishes.

KITCHEN EQUIPMENT

- Is there space elsewhere in your home for storing appliances? Could the washing machine live in a cabinet or under the stairs? Could the freezer be hidden under a tablecloth in the living room?

- Many small electrical appliances, such as hand blenders, are designed to be stored on the wall. Gadgets and knives can be hung on rails or magnetic racks.

- If counterspace is minimal, and you cannot live without your microwave oven, try storing it on a pivoting television wall bracket.

- Many sinks can be covered with a specially-shaped chopping board to give you a bit more worktop space. Similarly, if you are buying a new range, choose one that has a sturdy cover.

- Built-in appliances look sleeker than freestanding ones, but they are difficult to take with you when you move. They cost more, too. However, if the kitchen forms part of a larger room, it is worth buying appliances that can be fitted with fascia panels to match the units and create a more streamlined look.

- Runs of narrow shelving in the space between worktops and wall cabinets are ideal for storing small cans and packages.
- Concealed fluorescent strips beneath wall units keep work surfaces shadow free; ceiling fittings should be angled so that they clearly illuminate the insides of wall cabinets and shelves. Use shaded spotlights for the best effect.
- The door swing on large appliances such as refrigerators and dishwashers can create problems in tight corners. Some manufacturers have tried to overcome this by introducing pull-out models that operate rather like large drawers.
- Smaller-than-usual ovens are often multi-purpose, incorporating a microwave, a conventional oven, and a broiler. They can be built into wall or base units, and would need only to be combined with a two-burner rangetop to cover all your cooking options.
- All major appliances are available nowadays in compact or slimline versions. However, their size limits their suitability for large families.
- To save space, invest in a waste disposal unit and a trash compactor.

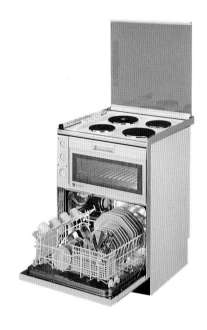

THINKING SMALL

The ingenuity of kitchen designers knows no bounds. A rangetop, oven, and six-place-setting dishwasher have been shoehorned into an area no bigger than an ordinary stove (above). The table (left) simply glides into the wall when not in use. Sometimes, there is simply no room for a separate cooking area, but there may be space for a galley in a corridor (above left). If you are able to accommodate a closet, you also have room for a kitchen-in-a-closet (opposite). Everything you are likely to need is in it.

LIVING ROOMS AND WORKSPACES

Whether you are relaxing or working, good seating and storage are the key to successful living rooms. As well as being the place where you spend most of your waking hours, living rooms also act as a buffer zone between the outside world and the rest of your home, so they need to be welcoming, flexible, and easy to use. Do not be tempted to over- or under-furnish this room.

Workspaces, on the other hand, can be either cluttered or minimal, but they must be designed with function in mind.

ROOM FOR LIVING

Living rooms, whether large or small, are often put to several uses, including watching television or listening to music. However, most of us eat, pursue hobbies, pay the bills, and even work in here, too, so furnishings need to be fairly hardwearing. And, as this is the most public part of a home, where we entertain frequently, and sometimes accommodate guests for the night, it should also be comfortable and adaptable.

Despite its many uses, the living room need not be the biggest room in the house. For example, you may be better off turning the main room into a combined kitchen and general family area, and devoting a smaller room to the hi-fi and television. Or, if you have more than one floor, why not site the living room on an upper level, where the availability of natural light and the view from the window are likely to be much better?

When space is at a premium, it is well worth trying to expand it. If there is an adjacent hall, how about replacing the wall between the two areas with decorative screens? This will make it feel less poky, while maintaining an all-important feeling of privacy. If the room leads onto a terrace, try replacing an ordinary door with French windows to make it feel bigger and brighter.

Once you are happy with the shape and location of the living room, it is time to sort out the contents. The most important of these is seating, as the room is primarily a place for relaxation. While the number and shape of chairs is a matter of budget, taste, and personal preference, a good starting point is to acquire at least one or two properly upholstered pieces. Two-seater sofas are a wiser choice than three-seaters, as they make it easier to experiment with the layout of the room.

BRIGHT LIGHT

Bulky furniture and dark, heavy fabrics can make small spaces feel even more cramped, so this top-floor apartment displays a light and less visually intrusive style of decor. The tubular construction of the sofa frame and dining table (right) allows you to see into every corner of the room, thereby making it seem bigger. The canvas and metal chairs (left and far left), whether spread out or stacked, take up very little space. Square parquet flooring set on the diagonal seems to push the walls outwards. And narrow shelves are used to display small objects, thereby reducing the need for space-hungry tables and bookcases.

Neutral colors and simple furnishings (previous page, left) come together to produce a soft, traditional look. Layers of fabric and other textural contrasts help to blur the edges of the room, while a lenient yet organized attitude to clutter pays dividends; books are stacked and collections are loosely grouped. However, the white-on-white scheme maintains an overall mood of crispness and calm. In the mini office (previous page, right), the same result is achieved with strict tidyness – perhaps the hardest decorating job.

COLLECTIONS

- Wherever possible, collections should be displayed on walls. Corner cabinets and shelves make good use of dead space and they keep fragile items safely out of harm's way. Alternatively, run a narrow shelf along the walls, preferably at shoulder height or above.

- If items are very small, try displaying them in velvet- or sand-lined trays. This makes them easier to move when you need the extra space. Old printer's typecases, which are shallow boxes divided into dozens of small compartments, also make good display shelves for tiny objects.

- Photographs and postcards look more decorative when displayed under a sheet of glass on a table.

- Use the tops of cabinets and book-cases to display one or two large objects. Smaller items are difficult to see when placed higher up, but a massed group of similar items has considerable charm.

Old dining chairs, floor cushions, and divans do not provide enough comfort and support for the average back if you plan to sit in them for any length of time. You are better off with wicker or director-style chairs, as these can also be used at the dining table.

You may find an upholstered footstool or ottoman useful, as it provides extra seating and storage, as well as a temporary home for newspapers and magazines. If this, or any other kind of low table surface, is to be placed in front of a sofa or armchair, try to leave about 18 inches of legroom; any less will make the area cramped and unwelcoming.

The dining table may have to double up as a desk and hobby area, so choose one that is stable and capable of withstanding regular knocks and spills. It should also make good use of space; a round table can be pushed into a corner when not in use, while rectangular trestle tables ideally suit hallways and narrow rooms.

Seating and storage should be combined wherever possible, but you will still need extra space for books, compact discs, and the other detritus of modern living. Freestanding storage can be used as a focal point or space divider, and it has the advantage of being portable when you move house. Built-in units, on the other hand, make the best use of space, and they can be tailored to suit your needs. However, they are also expensive, unless you opt for simple forms of open shelving.

Lastly, keep an eye on decorative clutter, as it can all too easily swamp a room. The secret is to organize it in the form of displayed collections or themed groups and to contain it in a limited area.

AWKWARD SPACES

Pale yellow walls provide a neutral backdrop for collected treasures, while maximizing the sense of space in this octagonal room whose diameter is only 13½ feet. A wicker sofa offers a lighter alternative, both in visual and practical terms, to traditional upholstery. And a carefully positioned table lamp helps to light up the darkest corner of the room.

Unusually shaped rooms have great charm, but they can be extremely difficult to furnish. The answer is to keep the walls plain and simple, and to draw the eye toward the center of the room, by using inviting and colorful furnishings. Mirrors are a great help, too; even an irregular room shape is improved by a little reflected symmetry.

GALLERY LIVING

A lowered ceiling and simple checked furnishings create an air of cosy seclusion in this comfortable living room, while the gallery above provides a touch of high drama.

Like all galleries, it acts as an oversized shelf, perfect for housing overnight guests or temporarily abandoned hobbies. A larger gallery might be used as a refuge or study. Even where ceilings are not this high, it may be possible to create a snug sleeping platform, with the space below it devoted to storage.

Galleries, like shelves, can be cantilevered off a wall, supported by beams and brackets, or suspended from the ceiling, as long as the loads are not too great.

CHARACTER PARTS

A careful choice of furnishings in a living room is often all that is needed to create the right mood. Here, a cottage living room has been given a casual yet pulled-together look by using the same fabric in several color-ways. All-over patterns such as this are generally better suited to simple schemes. Informally-placed accessories help to foster a mood of rustic calm.

Careful coordination is never the whole story, however: Successful rooms should also contain one or two surprises. Here, a steeply vaulted and beamed ceiling contrasts dramatically with the cosy furnishings below; the striped effect makes the ceiling seem even higher, and gives the room added grandeur. And a patterned carpet provides a pleasingly eccentric touch.

ORANGE AID

Simple decorative tricks are often the
most effective. Here, colorful furniture
and a dramatic orange screen in a top-
floor living room, focus attention on
the lower half of the room. The screen
draws the eye away from the low
ceiling and makes the room appear
more spacious, while the zingy color
scheme also helps to brighten up an
otherwise cool, dark room.

The screen is made from a timber
frame covered with plywood and its
shape both echoes the semi-circular
window and allows as much daylight as
possible into the kitchen. Set at an
angle to the wall, the screen creates a
"dynamic", helping to bring the space
to life, while making the living area and
the kitchen feel more enclosed.

SCREENING

- Some form of screening behind a sofa is essential if it sits, as here, in the middle of the room. But it does not have to be permanent. Paneled screens, or even a table that is as high and as wide as the sofa, would work just as well.

- Screens, whether movable or fixed, should stop well short of the ceiling so that daylight can reach every corner of the room, so as to prevent a feeling of claustrophobia.

- In a living room or workspace, use a paneled screen to define the space. Around a dining table, a screen will create a sense of intimacy.

- As an alternative to draperies, try unfolding a screen in front of the window at night. In an older house, full length integral folding shutters also are a good solution.

- Lengths of fabric or blinds hung from a ceiling make effective room dividers, as they can be tied back easily to open up the space. Use plenty of fabric for a generous effect, and make sure that the fabric can be removed for cleaning.

ELECTRIC CANDLESTICK

A simple candlestick fitting provides both task and accent lighting in this rustic living room (left). The shade directs light downward to make reading easier, and the pool of soft light it casts attracts the eye. When coupled with low-level backgroung lighting, the result is wonderfully relaxing. The contrasts of light and shade should not be too great, otherwise the effect becomes less inviting.

As with all light fittings, the correct positioning of reading and other task lights is crucial. If they are being used to illuminate a working area such as a desk, they should be angled so that shadows are cast away from the desk. The shade should sit approximately at eye level to reduce glare.

Lights that are sited next to an armchair or sofa should be placed slightly above the seating for dramatic effect. This works perfectly well as long as the bulbs are not too bright. You should also check that the faces of people sitting on chairs remain free of unflattering deep shadows. This can usually be avoided by carefully lining up the lamp with the front or back edge of the chair.

LIGHTING

All living rooms, whatever their size, play host to a wide variety of activities, all with different lighting needs. Moving around, holding conversations, and watching television need only a low but safe level of background light; reading, writing, and hobbies are made easier by localized pools of task lighting; while collections of pictures should be highlighted.

In addition, fittings need to be capable of creating several moods: You may want them to add cheer on overcast days, or to create sparkling glamour for parties.

It therefore makes sense to invest in flexible fittings. Those with dimmer switches make it easy to alter the mood. Other designs have movable arms or shades, which allow you to bounce light off the walls or ceiling.

Position lights correctly: The middle of the room is rarely the best place for a ceiling pendant fitting, as this creates shadows in corners. To "move" the pendant without expensive rewiring, simply attach a longer length of cord. This will let you position it over a table, or close to the wall.

Display lighting can emphasize specific items (above left) as well as draw attention to architectural features.

White surfaces bounce daylight into a room to provide cool background lighting (above right), which feels calm and refreshing during the day. At night, the atmosphere is warmed by recessed downlighters and a tall floor-standing candle stick.

WORKSPACES

We all need somewhere to store papers, bills, or an answering machine. Some of us can make do with a spare shelf or drawer, while others need much more space, perhaps a separate room. However, the ideal for most small-space dwellers is a table and chair in a corner: a place to think, make decisions, and dream.

Your basic needs are a table or wall-mounted surface that flaps down, plenty of shelves, and a folding chair. But it always helps if the space can be closed off or hidden in some way, so that work can be left out overnight. This needn't involve expensive building work; folding screens can be used to hide the mess, or it may be possible to tidy away current work papers behind cabinet doors in an alcove.

WORKING DAY

Living rooms, kitchens, and bedrooms are the most obvious places to site workspaces, but a stair landing (left) or lobby (right) will do just as well.

Anyone who plans to use their study regularly should also spend some time selecting the right table and chair. The latter should be reasonably compact and portable, so that it can be used elsewhere. And when you are seated, it should allow your feet to rest comfortably on the floor, with your knees very slightly lower than your hips.

The table or desktop should be sufficiently high to allow your legs to slip underneath. But it should still be possible to rest your hands on the top, with your arms relaxed by your sides, and your elbows bent at 90 degrees.

Strong, direct light, such as that provided by Anglepoise lamps (far left), is useful if you read or do close work for long periods of time. Otherwise, it is best to use lights that shine sideways onto the working area.

If you use a personal computer, do not place the screen in front of, or facing, a light source or window, as this causes glare. Again, it is best to light it from above or from the side.

BEDROOMS AND BATHROOMS

A bedroom is a private retreat, a place to relax, shed outer layers, and dream. As such, it can present complex planning problems: As well as being the place where you sleep and store your clothes, it often doubles up as a study or second living room. Sometimes an en-suite bathroom may be needed to relieve pressure on the rest of the house. Fear not: All this, and more besides, is possible in a small bedroom. Size really does not matter when you are creating and decorating the room of your dreams.

WHITE MAGIC

The space-expanding properties of white are well-known, but many people tend not to create all-white interiors, mainly because they have a reputation for being impractical. There is also an underlying fear that the results may look too clinical.

While it is true that all-white schemes do not suit busy family rooms, there is no reason why they should not be used elsewhere. This pretty bedroom (right) is decorated with several shades of white, ranging from pale putty on the floor to snowy gloss paintwork. Extra interest is provided by textural contrasts. A curvy upholstered chair is silhouetted against a Venetian blind, which in turn is softened by a loosely draped pelmet. Like most of the fabric in the room, it can be removed easily for cleaning.

Corner closets are unusual and decorative, and they often seem less intrusive in small bedrooms.

A low-level bed (previous page, left) helps to keep heads clear of the dramatic roof in a galleried bedroom.

In a tiny bathroom (previous page, right) a wall-mounted sink and mirror put an awkward corner to good use.

BEDROOMS

Beds and chests of drawers are often the largest items in the house, so it is very easy for small bedrooms to seem doubly cursed. But a lack of floor space can be an asset if you are aiming for a feeling of womb-like cosiness in the bedroom, and nowadays it is easier than ever to buy space-saving furniture.

The size and position of the bed governs most schemes; it is, after all, the focal point of the room. But it should not be chosen for its looks alone: The quality of the mattress and base, if any, matter just as much.

When planning the layout of a bedroom, you may well find that there is only one sensible place for the bed, against the wall. This can create a hemmed-in feeling and make the room look mean and cramped. But raising the bed, by siting it on a sleeping platform perhaps, makes a big difference; it increases the amount of floor space, and allows you to use the area below for storage.

Reducing the visual impact of the bed is also a good idea in small rooms. The easiest way to do this is to use some kind of foldaway. Sofa beds are the most common, closely followed by futons. In addition, there are several types of bed that will fold up and cleverly disappear into closets during the daytime, among them the charmingly-named Murphy bed.

Alternatively, box beds can be built into a wall of cabinets for a neat, nautically-inspired look. Making a box bed is a job for an experienced carpenter, but the end result looks wonderfully warm and secure and is especially suitable for children.

Color and decor play a large part in making bedrooms feel spacious; pale, soft colors and shades of white are the traditional choice in these circumstances, but an airy yet comfortable atmosphere can also be created with faded rich colors or warm, natural tones. The bedroom is a good place to experiment with large-scale patterns. They create an air of cosy seclusion, but may be oppressive in rooms that are also used during the day.

Bedrooms call for a large amount of storage space in which to house clothes and shoes, and many people automatically opt to build fitted furniture.

The great advantage of this approach is that it makes great use of space, and creates a smart, streamlined effect. But it is not a cheap alternative: All those accessories, such as shoe racks and sock drawers, cost extra money. Units at the cheaper end of the market rarely fit exactly, and you may have to assemble them yourself.

A cheaper, and often more satisfying, alternative is to design and build your own storage; this works especially well in alcoves, and on the end walls of narrow rooms. The entire surface can be covered with a tailor-made combination of shelves and drawers. The end result can be covered with sliding panels or blinds; these take up less space than ordinary closet doors and allow you a chance to experiment with color.

However, it is still worth including one or two free-standing pieces of furniture, such as a chest of drawers or dressing table. Most of us like to move the furniture around once in a while, and a surface on which to display favorite objects is a must, especially in traditional schemes.

BEDDING DOWN

You do not need to have lofty ceilings in order to enjoy the extra space created by raised beds. This studio ceiling (above) is less than 10 feet high, while the cabin (right) is on an even smaller scale.

   An air of other-worldly seclusion fills this room (opposite), thanks to a quirky use of polished metal panels and rich fabrics.

BEDS

■ A bed is the most important element in any bedroom, so always buy the best mattress you can afford. Turn it regularly to even out wear, and make sure that the underside is ventilated to prevent moisture build-up.

■ When buying a bed, remember that it may need to fit through narrow doors and around tight corners. Many bed frames can be taken apart for transportation.

■ The size of a bed makes it a natural focal point in a room, so emphasize it with a headboard or decorative frame. If floor space is very tight, hang a canopy overhead.

■ Try to leave a 2½-foot gap between your bed and other items of furniture. If wardrobe doors open into this space, the gap should be at least 3 feet.

■ It may be possible to buy a head-board that flaps open to reveal storage space within.

■ If you plan to build a platform bed, make sure that the floor can bear its weight.

MAGIC TRICKS

Alcoves and recesses make good
storage spaces as long as they are not
boxed in. Here (left), doors of any kind
would have looked clumsy, forming ugly
panels in the wall, and thereby jarring
with the room's elegant feel.

Draperies hung from a peg rail are an
excellent way of screening alcoves, as
they give the wall a sense of unity, and
add a touch of softness to a crisp,
architectural scheme. Matching them to
the paintwork maintains the feeling of
simplicity and keeps their visual impact
to a minimum. This soft, romantic and
ethereal look is delightfully easy to
achieve, but it must be kept
scrupulously clean.

To make the most of natural light, a
mirror is placed next to a window
(right). If this is not possible, try
cutting and framing a mirror so that
it echoes the shape of a window, and
hang it opposite to create a pleasing
symmetry. Mirrors, like pictures, can be
grouped on a wall or table.

STORAGE

- If there is room at the foot of the
  bed, use a blanket box or ottoman
  for storing out-of-season clothes and
  bed-linen.
- Bedside tables should incorporate
  storage wherever possible. The skirts
  of a fabric-covered table (left) are
  capable of hiding an enormous
  amount of clutter. Small chests of
  drawers and filing cabinets are also
  useful in bedroom settings.
- If floor space is very tight, fix sturdy
  shelves or decorative brackets next
  to the bed. They will look even
  better if your bedside lights are also
  wall mounted. Remember to leave
  enough room for moving the bed.
- A few items of clothing, such as hats
  and shawls, will form a decorative
  display placed on a stand or on the
  wall. A valet stand will help to keep
  clothes off the floor, as will a row of
  hooks hung discreetly behind a door.

■ 69

CLOTHES STORAGE

■ Store rarely worn clothes elsewhere, in an attic or landing closet perhaps, then group the remaining items in your closet, according to type and length.

■ Coats and dresses need 5 feet of hanging space, while shirts and separates will hang in 3 feet 3 inches. If possible, fix the rail at 5½ feet, and use the space underneath for a shoe rack, shelves, a drawer trolley, or stacking boxes.

■ A garment rack is much cheaper than any kind of closet. Buy the largest size that you can afford, so that there is spare rail space for a set of lightweight hanging shelves. These can be used to store shoes or folded clothes. If possible, hide the rack behind a screen or drapes when not in use.

■ Keep large and small items separate. Bulky woolens can be stored on open shelves or in boxes, while small items such as socks and underwear are easier to find in shallow trays or drawers. Accessories and jewelry should be kept in lidded boxes.

■ Fix hooks or rails to the insides of closet doors to hang ties, belts, and small bags.

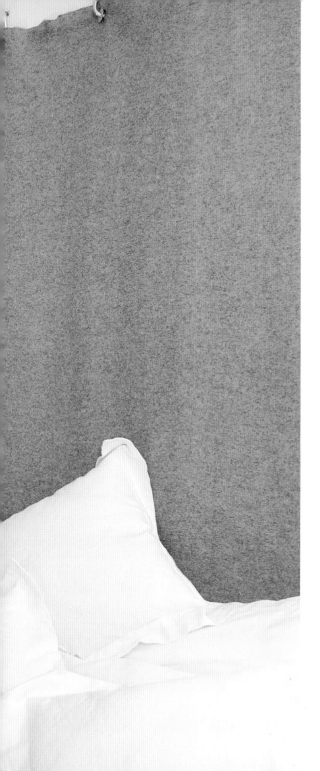

HUNG, STORED, AND QUARTERED

Open storage for clothes is often seen as an open invitation to dust, but it can make the most of limited space. Recessed and built-in shelves such as these (left) often make a pleasing pattern, and can therefore be left exposed. If you could never aspire to this level of tidyness, then cover the whole area by hanging a simple drape.

A more sensible compromise might be to mix open rails with drawers and boxes, as in this unit (above). Two sizes of willow basket keep clutter safely hidden from view. The only items left on show are those which have a pleasing shape or color.

BOXING CLEVER

Tongue-and-groove paneling adds a neat, cottage-like charm to an attic bedroom (left below), but it also serves several practical purposes. Imperfect walls and ugly pipes are concealed; there is greater insulation against drafts and wind noise; and the bed has been incorporated into the overall design – always a good idea in awkward spaces.

In a roof-top bedroom (left), a similar approach helps to turn an ordinary mattress into a multi-purpose piece of furniture. The area underneath the bed is divided into three cupboards to make for easy storage of smaller items, while the lower part of the wall behind is boxed-in to create a home for bulkier items, such as bedlinen. With a few cushions propped against the cupboard doors, the bed becomes a sofa. And the narrow shelf created along the top of the cupboard acts as a bedside table.

If carpentry is not within your range of skills, a similar effect can be achieved by resting the mattress on a platform made from modular storage boxes (right). Other low items of furniture such as architectural plan chests or metal filing cabinets could also be used as bed supports.

UNDER-BED STORAGE

■ Most divan bed bases have storage
facilities, usually in the form of
drawers or cabinets with sliding
doors. Other types require you to lift
the mattress up at one end to gain
access to storage underneath. The
former can be difficult to use in a
confined area, or if you have bedside
tables. The latter are best for storing
rarely-used items.

■ You may be better off buying a
slatted or sprung bed frame and
organizing the area underneath with
lidded boxes or suitcases. Color
coding and labels make it easier to
keep track of the contents.

■ Very low beds, such as futons, are
not so useful when it comes to
providing extra storage space, but
there are bases that incorporate
shallow drawers or space for storage
boxes.

■ Beds that incorporate storage can be
heavy, so take steps to ensure that
there is minimum damage to the
carpet or floor. It may help to fit the
furniture with castors. Drill holes in
the base to allow air to circulate
under the mattress.

BATHROOMS

Swimming pool-sized baths set in acres of pink marble exist only in the pages of romantic fiction, and given that they must take a small army of servants to maintain, it is probably just as well. Those of us who live in the real world generally have to make do with a great deal less space; bathrooms in some apartments can be as small as 24 square feet.

A miniscule bathroom can also be transformed into a luxurious retreat though. However, it does help if you are starting from scratch; only then can you choose the color of fittings and site them to make the best use of space. Pulling off the same feat with inherited fittings is more difficult (but by no means impossible). It just takes planning and a willingness to be inventive with color.

Drawing up a scale plan is vital for the design of a new bathroom. If you are unsure of your drafting skills, use the planning guide from a manufacturer's brochure. It consists of squared paper and cut-out cardboard shapes representing the toilet, showers, and baths. After marking out your bathroom on paper, use the shapes to determine the layout.

Although it is possible to move inherited fittings around, the job takes skill and patience, and it is rarely the cheapest option. Instead, build cabinets under the bath and sink. These will take up more space, but provide extra storage.

A fresh coat of paint makes a huge difference to all bathrooms (make sure that it is steam resistant, though). You can also distract the eye with murals and other decorative effects on the walls and ceiling.

CHROME WHITE

A row of aluminum-fronted cabinets (below and right) keeps bathroom clutter in its place. Walls tiled in a similar color create a streamlined look. A small wall-mounted radiator slots neatly under the sink, and helps dry towels on a swing-out rail.

Even if there is no room for a bath, there is always space for a shower. All you need is a tiled wall, a showerhead, and a hole in the floor (see page 14). Generally, however, shower trays are best sited in a corner (left), or built into a row of cabinets. Rigid enclosures look neater, and there is less risk of spraying the rest of the room, but shower curtains allow you to maneuver in tight corners.

PLANNING A BATHROOM

■ Try to position fittings near their relevant water supply or soil pipe as much as possible, but make an efficient use of space your priority.

■ Wall-mounted toilets and sinks will make the room look larger.

■ Most companies make scaled-down toilets and sinks, but these are not always suitable for daily use. Instead, buy a normal-sized model and save space in other ways, perhaps by choosing wall-mounted faucets, or a shape that takes up less room.

■ Proper heating and ventilation are vital, the former to make bathtime as much of a pleasure as possible, the latter to ensure that your decorative efforts are not ruined by the twin evils of odor and condensation.

■ Lights should make the room safe and comfortable to use. To avoid glare around mirrors, point light toward the user. Also, try to ensure that there is an even light for make-up and shaving.

■ Remember, electricity and water don't mix. There should be no naked wires, and all fittings should be installed by a qualified electrician.

PAINTED MINIATURE

Every spare inch of this tiny bathroom is covered with painted murals and is a brilliant success. Most people would be nervous about making a strong decorative statement in such a small space, but it actually makes perfect sense. After all, if the alternative is bare walls that close in on you, why not do something that is really worth looking at?

Fantasy decorative themes work well in bathrooms as they are occupied for a relatively brief period of time. And even the simplest of efforts make more of an impact in a small space.

However, it is important that richly decorated walls are clearly lit. Even in such a small space, a single overhead pendant fitting would leave much of the room in shadow, as dark colors absorb light. Here, the answer was to wash the walls with light from ceiling-mounted spots. White bathroom fittings help to bounce it into the corners.

REFLECTED GLORY

A large mirror can work wonders in a small bathroom. As well as stretching the space, and turning small groups of objects into impressive collections, it can be used by people of all ages. But there are limits to the amount of mirror a bathroom can take: Full-frontal reflections are not welcomed by all.

Replacing some of the glass in a window with mirrors will give you more privacy, but it greatly reduces the amount of daylight entering the room. Better to screen the window with blinds, as here. Alternatively, fix glass shelves across the window, and use the space to display decorative objects or steam-loving plants. Make sure that shelves can be removed for cleaning. If you plan to store everyday items such as toiletries here, check that they are within easy reach.

INDEX

PUBLISHER'S ACKNOWLEDGMENTS

We would like to thank the following photographers and organizations for their permission to reproduce the photographs in this book:

2 Mark Darley/Esto; 4-5 Simon Wheeler/Elle Decoration; 6-7 Casa de Marie Claire /P.Planells; 8 Tom Miller/Elle Decoration; 9 Scott/MarieClaire Maison; 10 Jean-Paul Bonhommet; 11 Marie Claire Maison/Tosi/Ardouin; 12 Richard Bryant/Arcaid; 13 IPC Magazines Ltd/Robert Harding Syndication; 18-19 Aldo Ballo; 20-21 David Parmiter (The London Studio of designer Martin Bass); 21 *right* Mark Darley/Esto; 22-23 Michel Fernin/Le Journal de la Maison; 24-25 Mark Darley/Esto; 26-27 Graham Henderson/Elizabeth Whiting & Associates; 28-29 Richard Bryant/Arcaid; 30 Paul Ryan/International Interiors; 31 Yves Duronsoy; 32-3 Trevor Richards; 36 Casa de Marie Claire/Stylograph/P. Planells; 37 René Stoeltie; 38 *above* David Parmiter (The London Sudio of designer Martin Bass); 38 *below* Ianthe Ruthven (Nicola Wingate – printroom and screen designer); 39 Mark Darley/Esto; 41 David Parmiter (The London Studio of designer Martin Bass); 42 Reiner Blunck/Abitare; 43 Simon Upton/Elizabeth Whiting & Associates; 44 Fritz von der Schulenburg (Juliette Mole); 46 Dia Press; 47 *above left* Abitare; 47 *above right* Rosieres-Conseils; 47 *below* Ornella Sancassani/Abitare; 48-49 Scott Frances/Esto; 49 Henry Bourne; 52-53 IPC Magazines Ltd/Robert Harding Syndication; 54 R.C. Stradtmann/Camera Press; 55 IPC Magazines Ltd/Robert Harding Syndication; 56-57 Paul Ryan/International Interiors; 58 Christian Sarramon; 59 *left* Lars Hallén; 59 *right* Paul Ryan/J.B. Visual Press; 60 *left* Ornella Sancassani/Abitare; 60 *right* Yves Duronsoy; 61 Ornella Sancassani/Abitare; 62 R.C. Stradtmann/Camera Press; 63 Trevor Richards; 66 *above* Aldo Ballo; 66 *below* Bo Appeltofft/Camera Press; 67 Fritz von der Schulenburg (Juliette Mole); 68 Camera Press; 69 Paul Ryan/International Interiors 71 Fritz von der Schulenburg (Richard Mudditt); 72 *above* Paul Ryan/J.B. Visual Press; 72 Dia Press; 73 René Stoeltie; 74 IPC Magazines Ltd/Robert Harding Syndication; 76 Jeremy Cockayne/Arcaid; 77 David Parmiter (The London Studio of designer Martin Bass).

The following photographs were specially taken for Conran Octopus by Nadia MacKenzie:
Courtesy of David Benson-Bunch 1, 3, 14-5
Courtesy of Gary Kang 7, 14-15, 40-41, 45, 50, 51, 64-65, 75
Courtesy of Nato Welton and Dawn Williamson 34-34

by Henry Bourne:
Courtesy of Johnson Naylor Design 16-17, 70-71

AUTHOR'S ACKNOWLEDGMENTS

A large chunk of the five years I spent at British Cosmopolitan magazine were taken up with finding small spaces such as these. My brief from editors Marcelle d'Argy Smith, Linda Kelsey and Rachel Shattock was to search out inspiring and accessible homes, and while it was rarely easy, their enthusiasm for my efforts made it all worthwhile. They too were inspiring and accessible, and I owe them more than thanks.

For opening their doors so willingly, and proving that it is possible to live stylishly in small spaces, thanks to Martin Bass, David Benson-Bunch, Wendy Greenbury, Brian Johnson, Garry Kang, Nato Welton, Dawn Williamson and all the other homeowners featured here.

Thanks to Fiona Lindsay at Limelight Management for doing the deal. And, for turning recce snaps and occasionally incoherent ramblings into a marketable product, many, many thanks to Jo Bradshaw, Helen Lewis, Jess Walton, Christine Wood and all at Conran Octopus. No control freak cum. author could wish for a better team.